Here at Dawn

Also by Beau Taplin

Bloom
Worlds of You

Here at Dawn

Beau Taplin

Andrews McMeel
PUBLISHING®

OPENING REMARKS

Ever since I was a young boy, I have sought out secret worlds; worlds of wonder and enchantment and beauty in abundance, where no pain or suffering would ever dare live. I would wander the mountains and forests and imagine playful lights dancing up in the treetops with such clarity I could swear they really were there. I would wish day and night that I might tumble down a rabbit hole and be spirited away on some fantastic adventure. As far back as I can remember, I have searched for the hidden magic in things, those moments that seem to glimmer and shine with their own inner light, and so my sole hope and intention with this collection of verses is to simply encourage you to do the same. To see how the rabbit hole, this deep magic, belongs not only to stories but also can be found right here beneath the soles of your feet, in the soft light of morning, amongst the woods and the streams, in dance, in music, or a lover's kiss. The message of *Here at Dawn* as I intend it is this: there is nothing ordinary about you or this remarkable world we inhabit. There is wild beauty, there is poetry, alive all around you. The secret is knowing where to look.

THE DEEP NIGHT

The next time
you find yourself in a dark place,
I would like you to step outside,
gaze long and hard
into the deep night,
and find comfort in the understanding
that the absence of light
makes nothing in this universe
any less astonishing
or magic.

STEADY LOVE

In this life,
a steady love
and someplace to call home
are far more precious
than all the earthly possessions
and wealth in the
world.

A NEEDLE AND THREAD

The secret is to never lose sight
of the simple, everyday miracles in life:
good food, literature,
laughter, music,
compelling conversation,
nature, and art.
Look for them in every day,
and even when it feels like your
whole world is unraveling,
you will never be too far from a
needle and thread.

YOU GREW IN ME A GARDEN, AND THERE LIFE BLOOMED LIKE SPRING

How do you know when you are truly in love?
You suddenly find more beauty
in even commonplace things:
sunsets, the stars,
birds diving in pairs through the trees.
You have this magnetic aura
about you that even strangers can sense,
and music permeates
your every last waking moment.
It does not feel like possession but rather
this deep, driving need to give the world to your person,
whatever, no matter the cost.

THE SYMPHONY OF THE EARTH

Your life is like a stone
skimming across the surface of a river,
its ripples reaching out gently
in every direction,
the influence of its impact extending further
than its size should suggest.
Should you ever begin to feel
like your life holds no meaning,
remember this: your simple presence
is an instrument in the symphony of the earth,
and every last soul note is needed here.
Every kindness you show others
passes on to another,
spreading and multiplying
like seeds on the winds,
and like this your spirit lifts all of the earth.
You matter.
You are valuable.
You have a role to play in the unfolding of all things.
Your life is not only your gift,
it belongs also to others;
you make the world a sweeter place
when you spend it well.

THE LINE OF LEAST RESISTANCE

Love,
like a stream of water,
will always follow the line of least resistance.
If you must force its path,
it's not meant
for you.

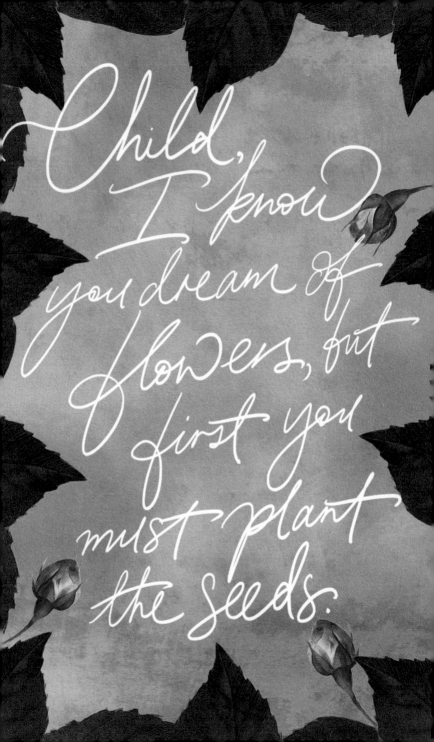

Child, I know you dream of flowers, but first you must plant the seeds.

TRUE FULFILLMENT

True fulfillment
is never found where you expect it to be.
When you most desire wealth,
you always feel poor.
When you most desire physical perfection,
you never feel enough.
When you most desire the love of another,
you only repel it.
And when you most desire success,
you always seem one last step from where
you feel you should be.
True fulfillment begins with celebrating
and showing gratitude for what you already have.
I am wealthy because I have life.
I am beautiful because I am human.
I am loved because I show love for myself.
True fulfillment begins with the perspective
that all you desire lives within you
and the understanding that the pursuits of your heart
are not work but play.

A RESOUNDING SUCCESS

Measure your success
only by what truly matters:
your happiness,
and the happiness you bring to others.
If today you laughed,
felt inspired,
or consoled a friend,
smiled to a stranger,
stood for a cause,
or inched closer to one of your dreams,
then today was a resounding success.

THE GIFT IN GOODBYE

When it comes time to say farewell,
whether to a love,
a home,
a path,
or a life,
let your practice be always the same:
just as we do in those final moments of light
beneath the late-afternoon sun.
Sit quietly for a moment, allow your heart room
to be heard, keep your breath steady
and centered as you reflect on the blessings
that have made this time in your life
so meaningful and precious.
Appreciate its place
and acknowledge its passing,
but trust also in the promise of new beginnings.
Where one chapter closes,
another begins.
Where there is falling light,
there is always soon a rising sun.
For all the hurt and uncertainty of now,
there are still bright days ahead.
However long and deep the night may seem,
the dawn always returns again.
The world will sometimes take from you
the very thing you can't bear to lose,
but if you listen closely to your heart,
if you look always for the light,
you will find it always offers something back.

ACT YOUR AGE

In a world where so much is expected of you,
one of the most important lessons you can learn
is that growing up doesn't mean leaving behind who you are,
that acting your age doesn't mean letting go of your youth.
The truth is, you are never too old
to dance in the rain until your skin turns blue,
to ride a bicycle through the night with the wind on your face
and all of your troubles long behind you.
You are never too old to blast the volume on your favorite song,
to mark your name into the wet concrete on the sidewalk
just because you want the world to remember you were here.
You are never too old to run away from home,
to put down all that is expected of you
and wander off lightly into the wild unknown.
You are never too old to rediscover yourself,
to dream and hope like anything is possible—it is.
You are never too old to make love like it is for the very first time,
full of nerves and clumsy laughter
and hands that don't know what to do with themselves.
You are never too old to take a chance,
to be as bold and reckless as you were with your heart
before years of rejection left you cynical and cautious.
You are never too old to reach out for help,
to fall apart gently in the arms of a friend,
to hold on to your mother like she is the last thing
anchoring you here to the earth.
You are never too old to remain young at heart.
While maturity may bring you wisdom and strength,
it is the playful, curious child in you that makes the world magic,
that makes a life enchanting and worth living at all.

AS NEATLY AS NOVELS

We demand closure
as though our lives
were put together as neatly as novels,
but the truth of the matter is they're not.
In real life,
relationships are messy
and poorly written,
ending too early or too late
and sometimes
in the middle of a sentence.

TAKE MY HAND

There is no reason to feel
troubled if your path
has not been made clear to you yet;
when you remain true
to your spirit and
courageous in action,
and listen ever to
the small guiding voice in your heart,
you find the universe
soon points out its place for you
and then leads you there
gently by the hand.

AND LET THERE BE LIGHT

There is still beauty
to be found in a bad day.
The difficult times are your defining
moments, and how they transform you is left
entirely in your hands.
What you choose to do with the hurt
you feel today can determine the happiness
you know tomorrow.
Let the pain be your power.
Let a fall be your fuel.
All light arises first from darkness;
this has been true of this universe since
its very beginnings.

Why should you be any different?

I HAVE SOWN FLOWERS DEEP
INTO THE EARTH OF YOUR MEMORY

Thank you.
Thank you for teaching me
where I draw the line between what I can forgive
and what I know I deserve.
Thank you for teaching me that poison
can be found on the tongue,
to trust in the honest labor of actions over
the honey-sweet sorcery of words.
Thank you for teaching me how to see through a mask,
to carefully unravel a clever disguise
and expose the true nature
concealed underneath.
Thank you for teaching me that
I can weather a storm
and still stand steady on my own two feet.
Thank you for every act of control and deception;
for each broken promise and
deep, cutting wound; for the lessons that now
allow me to know my own strength
and the difference between a flame that consumes
and a flame that just burns.
But I will never feel regret
for the bond that we shared,
for those sweet, tender hours we passed together,
for the love that we knew.

I have sown flowers
deep into the earth of your memory
to remind me that,
even in the most lightless
of places, beautiful things do grow.

DEVIL AND GOD

Yes, it is important to
be soft and kind
in the world, but it is necessary also to know
when to draw swords, when to fight
tooth and claw for what you believe in and love,
to balance the shadow in your heart
with the light.

As the rose is a rose for
both its flower and thorns,
the complete human soul is both
devil and god.

THE BLINDFOLD

When we fall in love, we are prone
to wilfully blinding ourselves to negative
qualities in our beloved we would
ordinarily find troubling.
We dismiss the complete picture and instead
choose the illusion, even when this illusion
begins to inflict us harm.
The only sight available to us not
distorted by these rose-colored glasses is the gut.
The lens of the intuition is exact and clear.
It sees all things only as they are.
Listen carefully
when it voices its warnings.
It sees truths your heart and mind
will not.

THE SEAFARING SOUL

In a soulmate,
we find a home here
on the earth, the final resting place on a
journey we travel all our lives.
While the stars that lead us together
may take their time, understand,
they do so always by design.
We have growing to do, after all,
challenges to face, an ocean to explore
before those golden shores are
ready to welcome us in.
And this ocean lies within ourselves.
We must take time to learn its waters,
its tempests, its treasures,
both its wild power and impossible depths,
and so when at last we arrive,
now seasoned captains of our own selves,
we know only smooth seas
together.

THE PROMISE

We are all taught to practice self-love,
but the crucial truth
is we have got to earn it.
Take responsibility for your poor habits
and work to overcome them.
Become someone you can trust in,
depend on, and admire;
someone you can feel genuinely
charmed to wake up to each morning.
Set the same standards
for your self-love
as you would for the love of another;
back up your words and your promises
with positive action.

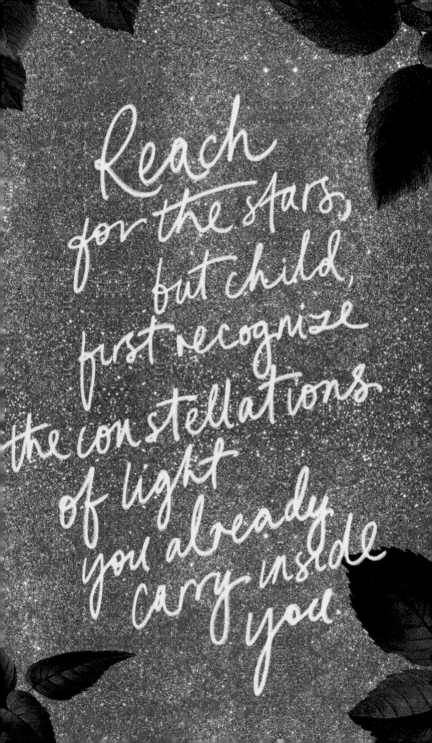

Reach
for the stars,
but child,
first recognize
the constellations
of light
you already
carry inside
you.

THE ROSE AFTER THE RAIN

When I think on the love we now share,
I am reminded of precious stones
shaped under the weight of a mountain.
I am reminded of roses blooming
all the more beautifully after the rains.
I am reminded of all sweet things
that are strengthened through challenge.
I am reminded of all the wonders of the earth
that would not exist without both night and day.
Because now, after all we have shared,
we stand by each other.
Because no matter the conflict,
there is always one constant: we always choose
to confront it, together.

THE MESSENGER

I understand too well how tempting it
can be to minimize or mask
emotional pain, to silence it with harmful
short-term escapes; but remember,
pain is only a messenger, one in the
service of our own subconscious,
pointing to a much deeper problem
in need of our attention.
And we do not shoot the messenger.
We must instead make it welcome,
allow it room to speak,
and through careful contemplation
provide it with a thoughtful solution that
might solve the root cause of the wound.
Pain is nothing more than
a weatherman warning of a coming storm,
a kindly neighbor trying to point out
a house fire in your living room.

Counterintuitive as it may sometimes seem,
your pain is here only to help you.

THE EVER-GROWING RIFT

I can see now
that the most awful of distances
is separated by neither land nor sea
but the ever-growing rift
between lovers once closely entwined.
It is a look of detachment
in your partner's eyes,
the slow extinguishing of a passion
that once raged like the sun.
It is to speak in a language of ever-deepening silence,
to sense a tender wound between you
and your beloved but feel so desperately
that you are unable to heal it.
But know this, my darling love: this is not who we are.
The roots of our love run deep and run strong.
We need only tend to the soil.
We need only remember the strength of our bond.
We need only remind ourselves of that small, fateful moment
when we found one another and all the world around us
seemed to bloom in response.
We are bound together, here at the heart.
We grow strong and flourish as one.
And before too long, I promise you this,
we will know the warmth of the
sunshine again.

GOLD IN DARK PLACES

Your life
is the one journey you will take in which
you can never turn back;
but if you keep your eyes facing forward,
if you keep your feet steady on the path,
you will soon learn this is
not such a terrible thing after all.
Life has a funny habit of hiding gold in dark places.
If you keep a patient heart,
your eyes wide open,
and trust in the long, winding road before you,
you see this life
doesn't necessarily reward those
who always make the right choices
but rather those who never stop
striving forward.

ONE SILVER LINING

Life doesn't play fair,
particularly when it comes
to matters of the heart.
Sometimes you will lose and
there is nothing that can
be done to prevent it.
You may be tricked, cheated,
betrayed, abandoned,
baited or broken, and then
left in the dark.
But while it is true these deep wounds
may come to define you,
there is one silver lining: you
decide how.

You alone
will determine what comes of this hurt,
let it sharpen you like
a blade.

WANDERLUST

The most liberating thing
about travelling alone
is leaving behind who others expect you to be.
When you are far away from the familiar,
your guard is free to come down.
You become a child again,
transported back to a time when all of the world
was new and each adventure,
each encounter,
revealed to you another fragment of your soul.
Travel builds character
because it serves as a reminder
that there remain mysteries in you still,
that the journey of self-discovery is always ongoing,
and it is only a plane ticket away.

SELF EXPECTATIONS

To bring a touch of beauty to the world while I am here.
Yes, that would be enough.

THE ARCHITECT

Trusting in the universe
means placing trust in yourself.
It is determining now, in this moment,
to fight on the side of your future,
to face all that has been holding you back
from claiming the life you desire.
Trusting in the universe
does not mean leaving your fate
to chance or the passage of time;
it is the faith that you have within you,
the capacity to improve your own circumstances,
it is the promise that you will one day
meet your true potential,
it is the understanding that you alone
are the architect of the universe you inhabit
and you are limited only by your
imagination.

TRANSCENDENT DELIGHTS

Meet with me
not only in body
but mind, heart, and soul.
Show me in your touch
what you can't find in words.
These desires of mine
demand transcendent delights;
when we escape together
to that tender, trembling place,
I am here to see who
you truly are.

When we meet together bound beneath the dark light of love, my body
speaking in tongues on the altar of your touch, and we travel where no
other has ventured before; all lovers past are in this moment forgotten
as we fold ourselves together into a form of our own. When we meet
eyes, our eyes meet only as they could. When our bodies fall and rise,
they do so to a rhythm known only to us. When your breath quickens
beneath my fingertips, yearning for that deep, silken place that will
drive you to climax, the song that escapes your lips is mine alone.
We drink deep from these streams that flow only between us. We
worship each other with burning devotion through our own
private rituals; my lips together in a kiss at the soft place your
thighs meet, one hand curled tight around your neck, the other met
in prayer at your rising breast. In each union, there is a newness,
an uncharted wilderness—like a snowflake or fingerprint, no two
are alike. When we surrender together in ecstasy, we craft our own
universe; when we fall into each other, we become gods.

THE CRUELEST TORMENT

I think there must be no
crueler torment
to the human heart
than to see an end coming,
as clear as morning,
but feel powerless to prevent it.

TRUE SUSTENANCE

Inner suffering is a hunger that
gnaws at the heart of you.
You can feed it material things,
temporary escapes,
even the love of another
and still find you are
left feeling starved all the same.
The only way to satisfy
its cravings is to search within,
to locate the greatest weight you can carry
and lift it, to root your purpose
not in what you can gain from others
but instead what you might give
in return.

THE FOG OF SORROW

When pain arrives, it shifts your perspective
on everything around you.
The days grow darker, the nights stretch further,
and you cannot, for the life of you,
find the light through the fog.
Everyday moments that were once beautiful to you
now appear colorless and dull,
and those songs that once sang full through your lungs
now serve only to remind you
of better days far behind you.
But don't lose hope.
Through these dark times,
you must simply learn to look harder for the light.
It will come to you in flashes
of unexpected beauty; the helping hand of a friend,
a compliment given or received,
a private moment of inspiration or peace.
Collect these tiny fragments of light wherever they come,
until at last your sky is so full of stars
you are finally able to see the way forward.

A TRUE FRIEND

Let this now
be a time to give thanks to
those true friends in your life:
those who applaud your successes
and soften your falls,
those who join you in joy through the highs
and tears through the downs,
those who point out the way
when you lose sight of your path,
those who accept you without judgment
and help you know your own light,
those true friends who, above all else,
inspire you to be a kinder friend
to yourself.

THE PIONEER

If you are having trouble
feeling present, stuck on autopilot
or disconnected, make
yourself uncomfortable,
throw yourself into the wild,
take chances,
risk failure,
find what frightens you
most and face it,
push back the boundaries of
who you believe you are.

You are a natural-born pioneer;
your adventurous spirit is a part of what
it means to be human,
as necessary to your existence
as nourishment or oxygen—it has coursed
through your veins
for over 300,000 years.

Why stop here?

THE MIGHTY OAK

No mighty oak grew
tall on her own.
She called on the winds to carry her seed,
the deep earth to settle her roots,
and the sun and rains
to make her strong.
We only flourish when we lean on each other.
This is how all great things
are grown.

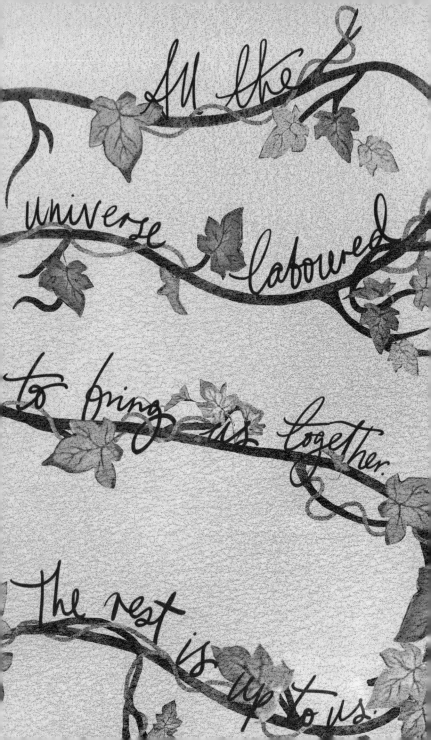

All the universe laboured to bring us together. The rest is up to us.

BENEATH A PASSING STAR

Now, like never before,
I know what it means to be understood,
to find oneself mirrored in another,
to speak in one soulful language,
to meet together so completely in truth and surrender
we melt like fallen snow into one.
I come to you now
in the knowing that all the world wills it;
the wild forests will green
as we lie bare beneath them,
the rivers will quicken
at the soft meeting of our lips,
the stars will sigh in
unison at our whispered confessions,
and even now, the winds carry me ever nearer to you.
Come to me now as you
have done endless times before.
I will gather together for you
all the flowers of the mountains
and lay them
here at your feet
just to welcome you home.
You are the wellspring of all beauty
and all things divine;
every dream I ever dreamt given form on the earth.
Until you are here,
I shall remain in this sweet unrest,
bound to you as life is bound to the breath.

TRUE LASTING HAPPINESS

True lasting happiness
cannot be found through
fortunate circumstances,
a positive mindset,
or even those you love and cherish.
Circumstances change,
mindsets can break, and your
loved ones may pass or slip away.

The solution: ground yourself
in a higher meaning,
commit your heart
to leaving the world a touch sweeter
than you found it, and then
plant your joy so deeply
in this purpose, no passing storm
can uproot it.

THE EVER-KNOWING SELF

You can be fooled
by your mind

and you can be
blinded by your heart;

the true answer
to any decision
lies always with the soul,

the divine intuition,
the ever-knowing self.

At times, we focus in on our problems at such a high resolution
they soon lose all discernible shape. We approach the question
from all angles, circling ourselves over and over, weighing the
possibilities of each outcome against all the others, until at last
we find ourselves back where we started: confused and undecided.
If you are here now in this place, gently close your eyes and journey
back to the beginning. Ask yourself the question one final time and
listen closely. The answer you are searching for will come to you in
one sudden moment;

hear it, trust it,

now transform into action.

The truth is, you have known
the right answer all along.
The true search is simply
finding the courage to own it.

THE WILDFLOWER

A wildflower
in a house garden
is only a flower; to claim you,
confine you,
or keep you for my own
would be to betray the very thing I have come
to adore most about you. If you
are ever to be mine, it will not be because
I have plucked you from the
earth for myself but because
I too have grown as
full and free as the wilderness,
and you have chosen
to grow here.

A SPRING MORNING DAY

Finding you
was like drawing the curtains
on a warm spring morning day;
a breath of light
and new beginnings,
as though the
world itself had been
remade.

FRAGMENTS

The difference between a broken heart
and a broken bone
is that when the heart breaks,
you decide how it heals.
Hard lessons don't have to leave you hardened.
These deep wounds are not
doomed to leave you with scars.
You may pick up the pieces
and plant flowers with the fragments;
who you become moving forward is always
your choice.

THE COMPOSER

Remember,
you are the composer
of your own life
and happiness.
If you don't like the music,
change the arrangement.

THE GREAT WORK

You are all the places you have been,
the sights you have seen,
the marvels you have achieved,
and every soul you have touched.
Each passing moment is
another brushstroke on the canvas.
So rise,
live always with passion and heart,
and someday you will look back on your life
and see a work of art.

Better an oops than a what if...

THE MORNING

The moment I met you,
it was like some veil in me had been lifted,
the world became brighter
and altogether more beautiful,
and the days
no longer felt so dull and drawn out.
It was as though
every moment before you
had been no more than a tiresome dream,
and at the sight of you,
the morning had dawned at last.

ONE SINGLE GLANCE

From the beginning
I had the feeling we had known
each other a very long time.
You could sense it in our body language
and see it in our eyes,
like whole lifetimes together
had been remembered
and relived
in the space of one single glance.

NURTURE YOUR CURIOSITY

Always hold this truth near to your heart:
whether you are the artist,
the mathematician, the entrepreneur,
or the gardener running your
hands through the soft earth,
nurture your curiosity, do not box yourself in;

read, write, stargaze, solve,
travel, illustrate, compose—explore.

There are an infinite number
of worlds on this earth, you need only
set off on the journey.

THIS PALE-BLUE DOT
IN THE STARS

When I say I think the world of you,
I really do mean the world;
every trickling river
and dark rolling sea,
the deep evergreen woods
and wild blossoms in spring,
white virgin snows on high mountain peaks,
sunburnt sands
and dandelion seeds on the wind,
the sleepy countrysides
and sleepless cities,
all of the earth's sacred places of worship,
the beasts and the birds,
every last daughter and son,
their every small wish
and their every great dream.
When I say I think the world of you,
I mean to say I believe you embody the majesty
of all that streams,
all that grows,
all that burns,
all that gusts,
all that falls,
all that passes,
all that has lived
and known love,
everything that is
or ever will be
on this pale-blue dot in the stars.

THE FIRST LANGUAGE

Love is a language in and of itself,
a language not made up of consonants and vowels
but truth, desire, and understanding.
When we love, we speak
in the ancient tongue of the stars,
we transcend the corporeal world
and enter a realm where the soul
may ask another to dance.
Love is to be seen and understood without
a single word exchanged,
to witness,
to learn,
and know another
in the space of one single glance.

THE GENTLE EMBRACE

In those joyless moments,
when loving yourself
feels impossible,
close your eyes,
visualize your arms extending
forward through time,
and gently embrace
the person you could be.

there is always a light
t the end of the tunne

You are the light at
the end of the tunne

There is always a ligh
t the end of the tunne

You are the light at
he end of the tunnel.

A SLIGHT MORNING FOG

Depression isn't always
a crushing weight
or a hand around the throat;
I think it's important to remember that.
For some, it is little more than
a slight morning fog,
concealing just enough light to spoil the joy;
never a sadness severe enough
to shatter the spirit
but one that saps slowly each day at your heart
until all of life is a cheerless
shadow of itself.

To these souls,
be a wind, a parting of curtains,
a reminder that just beyond those deep, rolling clouds,
there is still light;

there always is.

ONE SMALL GRACE

You may not always feel strong,
but you can always be brave;

again,

you may not always feel strong,
but you can always be brave.

SECOND THOUGHTS

In our final moments,
I am reminded of the silvery moon,
pale with longing,
admiring the falling sun from far across the sky
as it vanishes into the horizon.

In one last eruption of
light, you say your goodbyes,
and I wonder

why it is that all things of beauty
must be their most lovely the moment
before they are
gone.

THE FIRST LAW OF THE UNIVERSE

Before gravity first ruled what goes up must come down,
there existed a law of a greater nature,
known first in God's language as *Let there be light*
but put rather more simply as *What is must become.*
Since the very beginnings of the universe,
as the stars first scattered themselves
like golden confetti across the cosmos,
the universe has been in an unbroken state of becoming.
From vast spinning clouds of gas and dust, celestial bodies formed,
cells multiplied across primordial oceans,
the continents cracked and split,
mountains rose to the skies,
the wild trees spread their seeds,
and all creatures great and small learned to adapt and evolve.
From the mighty star to the humble rose,
the law of becoming guides all things in existence, and so
this must also be true of the human spirit.
In truth, we are all here to expand and transform.
It is in this elegant movement that we most closely mirror
the nature of the universe, and so it is here that we can
find most clarity and peace.
Look to your little corner of existence and make it sweeter;
in this simple endeavor you are doing the work of the stars.

ONE LAST ADVENTURE

All I have to survive
on anymore is this small foolish hope
that one day I will look up
to the sound of a warm, familiar voice
and it is you, after all
these long, unhappy years apart,
and with frail old bones
and wide wrinkled grins,
we will set out on one last adventure.

LILITH

To write of you is to write the truth,
to speak in the mother language of the moon,
to sing the spring songs of the flowers
in bloom.
You are a gift,
finely given,
from the heavens to the earth.
In loving you
I have learned I've loved no other before.
My sweet unbinding,
I have been made again in your arms.
You are the answer
to a question
I have asked all my
life.

AN EXTENDED HAND

Forget about pride and right or wrong,
if there is a wound between you and someone you care for,
you set aside your differences and heal it.

CRUEL INTENTIONS

Always observe and be mindful
of others' intentions toward you before you
allow yourself to dive in too deeply.
Some individuals are survivalists by nature and capable
of doing just about anything to get ahead.
To further their careers or
social status, or to feel financially secure,
they will abuse your tenderness and call it love.
The sad truth is, over time,
these individuals may come to develop
sincere affections for you,
but when you begin such a rare and beautiful thing
from such an insincere, ugly place,
it corrupts the relationship permanently.
Be authentic in love, always.
Be honest and kind to each other.
Human beings aren't rungs on a ladder,
and we never make it anywhere worthwhile
without true and meaningful connections in our lives.

IN THIS SILVERY MOMENT

Tell me,
how long do you hold on to a memory?
How do you decide
between the pain of remembering
and the pain of letting go?
What do you do with those slow,
sleepless hours,
the biting cold of an empty bed?
How do you carry the weight
hope leaves in the heart,
or the ghost of another's touch on your skin?
What do you do with the dream
of what might have been,
the sweet, stolen years of a life
you'll never know?
Do you fight it?
Do you pretend it away?
Do you place it down
in a quiet corner of your heart,
never to be seen
or heard from again?
I turn my eyes to the sun for answers,
and on the winds they arrive in the sound
of my voice.

Rise, she says, find your feet.

Stand steady in the promise all wounds do heal.

Be tender.

Be patient.

Find what little brings you joy

and let it gently fill your spirit.

Speak plainly.

Give your grief a voice.

Do not grant it strength through silence.

Let it sing.

Let it roar.

On those days you feel as though

you are falling backward,

know that even this is progress,

for the further away you move from loss

the deeper it will try to sink its claws;

but you will ignore these desperate pleas,

you will free yourself of all its chains

and know hunger in your heart again.

Breath by breath,

day by day,

strength will pour back into your bones,

your joys will grow,

these wounds will close,

and the horizon ahead will burn in gold.

And here,

in this silvery moment,

your heart will be returned to you.

At last,

in this silvery moment,

you will be ready for what tomorrow holds.

SELF-INFLICTED

I know it is my decision to sit in this grief,
that it is my fault alone.
I have been losing hours
looking back on where we went wrong
and tormenting myself wondering
whose body now lies next to yours,
but putting down this pain
would mean letting all I have left of you go,
and I'm just not ready to do that.

A SAFE HARBOR

I'm sorry.
I only ever wanted to be a safe harbor for you,
but I have storms of my own too.

love often and love deeply

COLLATERAL HEALING

Showing kindness
to others
is an act of self-love.
Every time
we lessen the suffering of another,
we alleviate
the suffering in ourselves.

DRAW THE CURTAINS

Today marks the day
that I return home to myself,
that I begin the long journey
that is beginning to trust in my own power again;
to engage life,
be light,
and stand confidently in my own skin.
And when I arrive,
I will move gently through each dark narrow hall,
and I will proudly draw back
the curtains.

TO LIFE ITSELF . . .

You have shown me
a free and boundless love;
a love that roams barefoot through the wilds,
a love that dives into the ocean
dressed only in moonlight,
a love that scales great mountains
just to howl to the heavens
and see all the world
stand still and breathless before it.
It is a love that dreams through the day
and stirs alive in the night.
It is a love that will never turn
away from a fight.
To life itself,
I commit my heart,
for in you I can always trust
to lead me back into your light
even when all else
seems lost.

FOOLISH GAMES

It's wonderful, isn't it?
All your life you let others into
your heart only to be
left disenchanted and hurt,
and so you let go,
lick your wounds, and
then begin all over again.
And on and on
these foolish games go,
until, one day,
you meet someone so
fantastically unlike all the others,
you forget there was ever
anyone else.

POLAR OPPOSITES

You and I
have always been polar opposites.
When I am east,
you are west.
When I am north,
you are south.
The differences between us
could span all the earth.
But when we embrace,
when we meet at the equator line,
together, we make a world.

A MATTER OF HEALTH

Whatever you decide,
don't stay because you are
afraid of change,
saying goodbye,
or ending up alone.
There is nothing more
harmful to your heart and soul
than sharing them with someone
not meant for you.

THE MONSTER UNDER
THE BRIDGE

Child,
you cannot escape your grief.
You can try to drown it in distractions,
numb it with your vices,
or even pretend
like it isn't there at all.
Sooner or later,
it will spring back
out of its secret hiding place
and demand you stand and face it.

A REASSURANCE

After a sad farewell,
there comes a point when
every one of us
questions whether love is really worth
all the pain and the loss.
The answer is yes.
Exhale.
It always is.
And in time you will know its
touch again.

FOLLOW YOUR PASSIONS

Follow your passions.
It is absolutely essential you discover
a way to obtain the same level
of satisfaction from your work as you
do from your free time.
To live only for the weekends
is, after all, to waste over two-thirds
of a life.

And you deserve a life lived in full, not only in parts. But living passionately doesn't mean we all need to be artists or entrepreneurs. There is meaning and magic to be found in all human endeavors; shopkeepers create community, craftsmen construct the homes that carry our stories, bartenders and waitresses help stoke the flames of young romance, and our teachers sow the seeds of all achievement on Earth. Living passionately can simply mean a shift in perspective: imbuing thought and feeling in all that we do and identifying what it is in our occupation that brings beauty to the world. Let all you do day-to-day be soul-sustaining work; life is too precious for anything less.

A MASTERPIECE IN PROGRESS

The makeup of your character
is not a puzzle with a set number of pieces.
All of the journeys you take,
the challenges you meet,
and connections you share in
over the long course of your life
weave another thread
into the fabric of who you are.
The work of self is never truly finished.
You are a masterpiece in progress.

DEPTHS AND TIDES

My love
does not come to those
who linger safely
by the shore.
Meet me down amidst
the depths and tides or don't
bother at all.

IN TIME, THE SUN DOES
RISE AGAIN

Following the loss of a loved one,
let this always be a reminder of one simple truth:
there is always hope, even here.
Embrace the healing hand of grief;
bear its weight as long as you need to,
but nurture your heart and take solace in knowing
that the pain and sorrow you are feeling
are proof you have known something sacred.
That the love you have shared
together will live on through you always.
Sometimes in tears
or a sudden ache in the heart
but also in those moments that move you
or bring you to laughter.
I will not say the loss will leave you unchanged,
but little by little, day by day,
all of the beauty of the world will begin to return.
Your heart will mend, the clouds will recede.
In time, the sun does rise again.

You will always
be the folded
page corner
of my story.

RAINCOATS

I hope you never steal someone's heart
just to fill a hole or heal a hurt.
A person's love is not a raincoat you slip on
only when it storms.

FAMILY TIES

Family is something
that runs deeper than blood.
It is nothing so trivial as a shared surname
or close physical resemblance
but this bone-deep sense
that you have an anchor
here in the world, no matter how far you feel
you have drifted off course.

THE UNWRITTEN NOW

Your past is a story that is already written;
you may thumb through its pages
and revisit the joy or the pain,
but you can never alter the story it holds.
Your future is a fiction fated to
remain forever unfinished;
however far along you might come,
you can never seem to complete it.
From time to time,
you may choose to explore it,
but if you dedicate yourself to it entirely,
you will never know what it means
to feel simply content.
But the present moment now in front of you
is a clean white page,
and here there are worlds to be discovered,
wisdoms to be learned,
stories inside of you just aching to be told.
Here in the unwritten now,
you are the author of your story,
and in the same way a simple sequence of words
can be woven together into a passage of elegant prose,
each passing moment has its place.

WHITE FLAG

Fight hard and fiercely for the one
who you love,
but after a point,
for the good and peace of your own heart,
you must learn to concede
defeat and withdraw,
to recognize clearly
when the war you are bleeding for
has already been fought
and lost.

THE SWEET ESCAPE

All of us are looking for some kind of escape.
Occasionally, we find it in each other.

DUSTY OLD LENS

There are times I feel like I am not wholly here,
like I am looking in on my own life
through a dusty old lens.
I can make out the outlines
of the things and the people I love,
but for the most part, it is all a shadowy blur.

STARTING OVER

Starting over needn't mean something so dramatic
as relocating your home
or switching careers
but can be as simple as resolving
to reject harmful energies,
abandon unhealthy habits,
or reevaluate your life vision.
It is simply drawing a clear, deep line in the sand
between you and what no longer
serves you.

THE SLOW DANCE

A relationship is like a slow dance;
every movement must be taken carefully
and in consideration of your partner,
and a single misstep can result in disaster,
but when a couple dedicates themselves
to perfecting this performance, to the
pursuit of intimately knowing each other,
the result is devastatingly beautiful.
Here, compromise and self-sacrifice meet
together like hands clasped,
trust and loyalty lock like a lover's gaze,
while a shared understanding meets every
coming challenge and conflict
with the mastery and grace of a dancer's step.
As one partner bends, the other bows.
As one partner falls, the other reaches out to catch her.
When a relationship works, it is effortless
and fluid, a meticulously choreographed pirouette
between two partnered souls in
perfect balance.

settling for something

that does not make you happy

is like diving

underwater for air.

UNWELCOME

Love is only a weight
when it is not yours to hold.
However deep or true
your affections,
there is no sense in devoting your love
to someone who is simply
unready or unwilling to receive it.
Direct your energies
where they're welcome.

ALL IS FAIR IN LOVE AND WAR

As the old saying goes, all is fair in love and war.
But we can still make the choice to be better,
to stand above it,
to let the heart of all places
be one of selflessness and truth;
to treat others only as we would like to be treated
and not play selfish games
that inflict pain just to distract ourselves from our own.
We can be dignified.
We can set a shining example.
We can better respect ourselves by showing respect to others.
Be honest, always.
Nothing lasts forever,
but if we are warm of heart,
then we can leave those we have loved
with a more positive lesson than simply what to watch out for.
In essence: when those who have
known your heart look back on their time with you,
let them find only light.

THE ASCENT

Perhaps you are not yet where you feel you should be, but from one dreamer to another, a careful word of advice: you could reach every last one of your goals and still find yourself miserable at the finish line. The true essence of life exists in the between. It is in the striving that your excellence is exposed to the world. It is in the setbacks that the strength of your spirit is learned. In the unfinished dream lies the full and burning heart of life. It is only a spell of the mind, an artful deception, that you might find fulfilment in fortune, fame, perfection, or power. Life is lived here, in the distance you have still left to travel. This is where the true magic happens.

TRUE APOLOGY

Consider this,

a true apology is composed
of actions, not words,

and one who is unwilling to
make amends for the wrong they have done you
is certain to inflict harm
again.

AN AWFUL WEIGHT

There is a small space
in my heart I have named after you.
I carry it with me
everywhere that I go.
The awful weight of what almost was.

WOUNDED BEAST

Take care of your loved ones,
particularly when they are doing everything
in their power to push you away.
A broken heart,
like a wounded beast,
will often lash out at those it is nearest,
but that does not mean they
don't need you.

HOSTELS AND HOMES

By all means,
go out into the world
and explore with your heart.
Fall in and out of love
until your hands are libraries of all
those they have touched.
Before long,
we all learn,
right down to our bones,
that some people are hostels,
and others are homes.

THE WIDENING VOID

This is when you know it is over,
when you find yourselves
constantly scrambling
for something, anything,
to hold on to,
when every kiss,
sorry glance,
and gentle graze of a hand
feels like you are
calling out to each other in desperation
from far across the stars.

THE HIGHEST LOVE

There is no higher love
than one you simply must be your most for,
than a love that awakens your spirit
and lights a fire beneath you
but welcomes you in only once you
have closed all wounds
and reached a place of quiet fulfillment
within your own heart and soul.
For this is the love
that allows you to bring
the most good and beauty
to the wider world around you;
and if love does
have a purpose greater
than simply bringing two souls together,
there is no question, it has got
to be that.

THE MAGIC TRICK

The truth is,
every last soul here is magic,
but still some of us choose to be the illusion of it.
We shroud our true selves
in a careful disguise
of what we believe others
will find charming or attractive,
hoping our audience will be impressed
by the performance.
But this has always been our mistake.
It is who we really are that is truly enchanting.
It is daring authenticity
that we have all arrived here to see.
You are not the magician,
you are the magic.
Before it is too late,
set aside the smoke and the mirrors,
allow yourself to be simply the miracle you are.
Set down at last the mask of self-distrust,
and see how all the world
cheers and applauds in response.

THE TRUTH OF GREATNESS

It is a simple thing
to get lost in the success of others
when a window to all the world
now rests at your fingertips;
but understand,
behind all greatness
there lies a long, painstaking process,
one full of missteps,
deep feelings of failure and doubt,
days you nearly give in,
and then days you fight forward
with every last ounce of strength in your heart.
Remember this the next time
you feel jealousy begin to claw at your chest.
The long road to our dreams
is a demanding one for all of us.
You cannot afford to expend your energy on envy;
you will need all the strength you can summon
for your own journey ahead.

THE GARDEN

Your soul is your garden;
you determine what grows here.
Cultivate courageous,
self-loving, and encouraging thoughts,
for these are the seeds
that will see you flower and flourish,
while bitterness, fearfulness,
despair, and self-doubt
should be stamped out at the root
like a weed.

Practice this,
and even when the world
around you turns cruel and unkind,
you will always find
within you a refuge of quiet beauty
and peace.

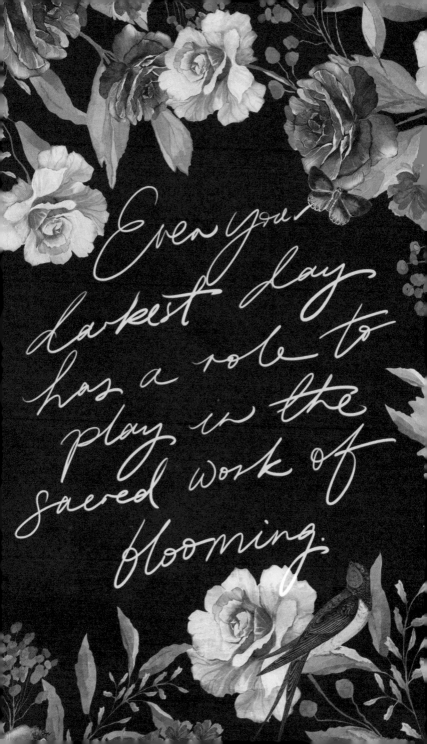

Even your darkest day has a role to play in the sacred work of blooming.

A SHIPWRECK IN A STORM

That is the exhausting
fact of moving on,
the relentless ups and downs,
your moods endlessly swinging from
one extreme to another.
One moment you feel the wind in your sails
and all the world at your feet,
and the next, you are a shipwreck
in a storm.

THE WANDERINGS OF THE HEART

As you gather up again
the tired pieces of your heart,
I hope you find small comfort in this:
every lesson you have learned
through those who have harmed you
has been guiding you
ever nearer to the one you are
meant for.

In the wanderings of the heart,
it is your losses that light the way forward.
One day, you will find
all you have been searching for,
and when this day comes,
you will look back
on these long winding roads you have travelled
and you will feel grace for even
the pain of this moment.

MANTRA

In those times
you are feeling lost or disheartened,
speak these words from the floor of your heart:
even here I am growing.
Even unfinished I am a story worth telling.
It is not where I am on my journey
that determines my value
but the courage it has taken
and my commitment to traveling
a little further along this road every day.
I acknowledge that we all
drift through seasons of shadow and light,
and so in this moment I will tend only to the spaces in me
that most need my attention and understand
this alone is a leap forward in a positive direction.
I will not let the pursuit of perfection steal away my present.
This is the most precious resource I own.
I instead resolve to rejoice
in this moment,
knowing I am doing my finest,
that I am striving forward and that is always
enough.

THE TRUE VALUE

The true value
of life
is not measured
by what we leave behind
but how fiercely
we love
and are loved in return
while we're here.

THE MOTHER AND THE FATHER

Our need for parenting
doesn't stop when we come of age,
the responsibility just becomes our own.
Show the child in you
tenderness through times of pain
and discipline when you lose your way.
Learn when to shelter
and when to let be
and nurture a careful balance
between work and play.
Instil in your own heart the strength
to both strive and succeed and the courage
to pursue your every last dream.
Treat yourself as you would
your own daughter or son;
when your inner child cries out
in need of guidance,
turn to the mother and father
within.

A VILLAIN AND A FRIEND

While doubt destroys,
failure frees.
While doubt confines you
to your comfort zone,
failure calls on you to confront
and transcend it.
While doubt discourages you
from admitting your affections for another,
failure brings you the lessons
that better prepare you
for the one you are meant for.
While doubt deters you
from pursuing your wildest dreams,
failure rewards you with the strength and wisdom
you require to reach them.

While doubt is a villain,
failure is a friend.
One must be firmly rejected
but the other
always
warmly embraced.

when you
bury the pain
you only
strengthen
its roots

THE DOORWAY

There are an infinite number of ways to lose someone you love. It could be to disloyalty, abusive behavior, tragedy, or even the cold, cruel march of time, but no matter the cause, the aftermath is always the same: you feel like you are at the point of breaking and the only one who can hold you together is gone. With nothing else to hold on to, you cling to the memory and make a home of a ghost, mourning every passing moment driving them further from you as days turn to weeks and weeks turn to months.

Welcome, this is rock bottom; but what you may have forgotten is that rock bottom is the foundation on which you can be remade. The truth is, all pain can be reshaped and repurposed. With the right care, all wounds will heal back more resilient than before. When the heart is shattered, you can create something beautiful from the fragments. Where there is some lesson, there is never a loss.

Listen carefully to your healing. Allow it room to do its work. Give yourself permission to feel grief when it calls on you to but also joy in those rare moments warmth returns to your heart. When you make the choice not to fight the currents of your feelings, you allow them to take you where they need to and so moving forward becomes a gentler process. Embrace your sadness, meet it head-on; it is a source of strength that can be drawn from and directed wherever you choose. Harness it as fuel for your dreams or a life change you've been neglecting. Loss will reshape you either way, but you alone decide what shape it leaves you in.

Remember always to move at your own pace. When you attempt to hurry yourself through a loss, you don't escape the grief, you bury it, and one day it will find a way back to the surface. Only you can know the distance of your healing, and only you can know when you have arrived. Be patient, be tender, and draw your strength from where you can. Your pain doesn't have to be your prison—remember that. It can be a key to a doorway, and you decide where it leads.

FRAGMENTS OF ONE FORM

You and I
are true counterparts to each other,
this is how it has always been.
The sacred masculine
and divine feminine
embraced in their eternal dance.
You are the birds above,
and I am the beasts below.
I am the pale light of the moon,
and you are the warm shine of the sun.
You are the melody,
and I am the rhythm keeping time.
You are the free wild seas,
and I am the sure steady earth.

In love,
we become fragments
of one form.
We are bound together,
as constellations are.

HERE IN THE SOFT EARTH

Love is grown as a seed is sown:
fragile at first and seasoned only through time,
the time to learn one another,
to deepen trust,
to form roots,
to learn how to endure the rains
and move again with the winds,
to soak in the sunshine
wherever it falls.
The time to tend with great care
to this young but flourishing love every day
until at last it is strong enough
to stand on its own.
We all dream of a love as full and free as the forests,
but first you must meet together,
here in the soft earth,
and allow it the space to grow.

RISE ABOVE

When you are mistreated,
rise above it,
set a shining example,
become such a force of warmth
and light in the world
that those who mean you harm
are blinded by your courage
and kindness.

A BROKEN HOPE

There must be
no more heartbreaking love
than one that never sees its moment
in the sun; than one stolen
from you before it even begins.
It is a kind of death in which you are left carrying
the weight of memories that never were.
It is a broken hope, a what-if
that lives always in the back of your throat,
a ghost that trails you around,
wherever you go, singing a tender,
haunting song.

THE SAFEKEEPING

It often strikes
in late and lonely hours,
the temptation to share your true feelings
with a love who is lost to you now,
to write them, to express how terribly they are missed,
how you can hardly suffer
another moment without them.
But do try to hold back.
When you open up your heart like this,
you are handing over a part of yourself, and
when your affections cannot be returned,
you don't get it back.
This can only prolong your pain.
It is healthier to hold on to these feelings
when you know they're unwanted,
to let them pass through you as long as they need to;
and then when they are ready to leave,
you gently let them go.

A SOFT LANDING

When you are falling,
the only one able to truly soften your landing is you,
so when you are trying to reach someone
who is caught in a dark place,
your only course of action is to help them
strengthen the light in themselves.
You can help point out their path forward
and even walk alongside them, but
you mustn't carry them no matter how
powerless they seem.
True care is not shielding a loved one
from their pain, it is helping them see they have
strength enough within them to confront
it themselves.

A REASON TO REJOICE

It is always a grace
to meet with another in love.
Even should the time come to part ways,
there is still reason to rejoice,
for the reflective gaze of love unveils
and shapes you; it invites you to bear witness
to your faults and to better
harness your strengths.
And so no time given to another
is ever misspent; should the love you share
reach a natural end, all you have
known together will be woven
back into the fabric of who you are,
leaving you with both lessons
and warm memories that will serve you all your life.
Even as your heart now aches at their leaving,
understand all you have shared in
has been a gift; this encounter between you
has left you forever transformed,
and like this, those you love
become a part of you,
so no one who has known your heart
is ever truly lost.

THE IMPERFECT COMPUTER

Your mind is an imperfect computer.
Your trials and traumas
will install with faulty software all throughout your life.
But remember this,
you remain the hands at the keyboard.
Our minds aren't who we are.
We all know this intuitively to be true.
Our minds are simply tools we use to express ourselves
to the external world, to measure and navigate it,
and ponder our place in it.
But like all tools, our minds
can at times fall into disrepair;
they can become corrupted by poor habits or past traumas,
particularly from our childhoods,
and stop serving us the way they are supposed to.
Recognize this when your mind next
calls you worthless, useless, or ugly—these are
nothing more than malfunctions in your system.
All of your fears and self-doubts,
they are just junk on your hard drive,
and you have the authority to remove them.

DEEP ROOTS

I plant roots so deeply
in the people I love
that I always lose a piece of myself
when they go.

JOURNEY SLOWLY NOW

Journey slowly now.
You have already come so very far,
but now it is time
to savor the views,
to discover new lands,
to turn your eyes to the stars,
to unearth the truth of who you really are;
to recognize there is both
a time to hunt
and a time to take rest,
and the sweetest of all earthly treasures await those
who look ever to the flowers
that bloom underfoot
and simply find joy in the
journey.

WILD GROWING THINGS

Go to the wilderness when you are in need of guidance.
Walk with light steps through the wildwoods
and witness firsthand
the greatness that can spring forth from
even the smallest of seeds.
Look to their curled branches and
observe how they ascend
always toward the light of the sun.
Sit by the rivers and streams and study
how they flow freely no matter
the obstacles that lie in their path.
Seek out the flowers in the meadows and see
how they never strain for their beauty,
how they focus only on blooming, and so beauty finds them.
The earth is a fountain of wisdom and knowledge
if only you can learn to speak
in her old language again;
wander free and far and look to all wild growing things,
for they are Her loving word
given form.

A WORLD BETWEEN WORLDS

For as long as I can remember,
I have found myself most drawn to those
who are able to bring me
out of my own world,
to those who might show me
a simpler,
more earthly place;
a world that may at times seem
a touch less enchanting,
but one where I would no longer feel
so isolated or alone.
It is as though all my life I have lived
in a world between worlds,
looking ever to the love of others
to deliver me back to the embrace of the earth.
But with you it is different.
You don't take me someplace else.
You meet with me where I am
because we are of the same world.
You too see the beauty
that blossoms ever in the deep.
We travel together down hidden paths
I have long thought my own.
You speak fluently the old language of my spirit,
and the song of your heart is one
I have always known.
For once in my life,
love is no longer an escape from myself
but instead a flame that bathes all my soul in its light.
In our world between worlds,
we dance embraced,
suspended together in a silvery twilight.

THE GAZE
OF THE PHOENIX

I meet your gaze
and something
with the shape of recognition
surges between us;
some long
forgotten history
hidden just beyond thought,
demanding to be
remembered.

In the space of an instant,
I am consumed
then reborn;
before I can come
to my senses,
I have already shed
the shell of my long solitude
and stepped into
the arms of another life.

TIME BENDING

It's a known truth
that all time is relative within
the chambers
of the human heart.
Consider the tender sweet
moments,
like those shared
with a lover or friend,
and their manner of speeding by you
in the space of an instant.
Consider those cold, loathsome
moments
that follow a final farewell,
that always seem
to stretch on for an
age.

A QUIET ACKNOWLEDGMENT

In this quiet moment,
I give myself permission
to acknowledge my progress,
to focus less on the distance
I've still left to go
and instead on the mighty distance
I've come.

THE TURN OF THE SEASONS

The soul moves
through seasons too.
And like the seasons of the earth,
each is as essential as the last.
The soul in an endless summer would
soon grow lifeless and dull.
We require the falls to shed those
things that no longer serve us;
we require the winters
to make way for new life to
bloom.

AN AUDIENCE OF ONE

In times of heartache,
there is no power
in pretending
you no longer care.
All healing must begin
with recognition of the wound;
let it out
in silver tears,
sing it from the rooftops
if you have to.
You are only
punishing yourself
hiding behind a performance
for an audience
who has already left
the room.

THE BOUNDLESS SELF

I see now that the purpose
of self-progress
is not to pursue perfection
but to move closer to the truth
of who we really are,
to untangle our deepest fears and doubts
and arrive in that tender, blissful place
where we are free to be
our purest, boundless selves.

VERSES OF BIRDSONG

Every so often,
may you rise before dawn,
before even the
verses of birdsong begin
and the first streams of sunlight
run their hands through
the trees,
before the mad rush
and burden of daily demands,
before a material world
can twist and tangle your thought;
may you stir awake in
the sweet hearth of the night,
when the deep, dreaming quiet
still reigns over the earth,
and the song within your soul
is free at last
to be heard,
rising to awareness
with the soft light of the sun.

INDEX OF TITLES

ACKNOWLEDGMENTS

All works of art and literature are as much creations of their audience as they are of their authors; the same way the true beauty of a forest is formed in the eye, this book is not a finished work until it has arrived in your hands, until you have folded the corners of its pages and underlined your favorite passages, until you have read it by night or shared it with friends, until it has been loved and worn and then finally passed on. It is you, my treasured reader, who brings this collection beauty and meaning, and so I dedicate it to you.

I would like now to thank my mother, who kindled everything worthwhile in me; my brave brother Jay, for his insight and strength; my father and all my extended family; my one Alizé, for finding me on the earth—in loving you I have wandered into a dream from which I will never wake. And finally, arranged in no particular order, I would like to thank Joel, Geoffy, Ben, Leon, Dave, Mikka, Michelle, Shea, Bec, Raissa, Jeremy, Stavros, Jessica, Brett, Matt, Jaxon, Tommy, Sophie, Sabrina, Anita, Montana, Nina, and Tanelle: whether what we share belongs now to the past or continues still in the present, you have all played a role in this past chapter of my story, and so this book is yours as much as it is my own.

I would also like to thank Lucy @lucyjanebrand for this collection's design, Sanda @broken_isnt_bad for its logo, Jess @altrd.studio for the typography, Ryal @ryalsormaz and Shea @sheachristie for the photography, and Kelly @kellymaker and Marta @carta_9169 for the beautiful artworks contained within. It has always felt important to me that a book's design should reflect the spirit of the writings it contains, and you have all done marvelous work; more than any other, this book captures my inner world. Anyhow, if you have made it this far, then all my love and warmth to you. If you have unearthed here even a touch of light, then this book has done its work.

Here at Dawn copyright © 2020 by Beau Taplin. All rights reserved. Printed in China. No part of this book may be used or reproduced in any manner whatsoever without written permission except in the case of reprints in the context of reviews.

Andrews McMeel Publishing
a division of Andrews McMeel Universal
1130 Walnut Street, Kansas City, Missouri 64106

www.andrewsmcmeel.com

20 21 22 23 24 SDB 10 9 8 7 6 5 4 3 2 1
ISBN: 978-1-5248-6167-4
Library of Congress Control Number: 2020933541

Editor: Patty Rice
Art Director: Diane Marsh
Production Editor: Elizabeth A. Garcia
Production Manager: Cliff Koehler

ATTENTION: SCHOOLS AND BUSINESSES
Andrews McMeel books are available at quantity discounts with bulk purchase for educational, business, or sales promotional use. For information, please e-mail the Andrews McMeel Publishing Special Sales Department: specialsales@amuniversal.com.